WRONG WAY

David Scott

authorHOUSE®

AuthorHouse™
1663 Liberty Drive
Bloomington, IN 47403
www.authorhouse.com
Phone: 1 (800) 839-8640

Published by AuthorHouse 12/08/2015

ISBN: 978-1-5049-6680-1 (sc)
ISBN: 978-1-5049-6681-8 (e)

Library of Congress Control Number: 2015920255

Print information available on the last page.

Any people depicted in stock imagery provided by Thinkstock are models, and such images are being used for illustrative purposes only. Certain stock imagery © Thinkstock.

This book is printed on acid-free paper.

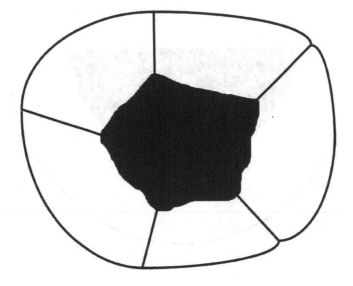

The wrong way to eat a banana.

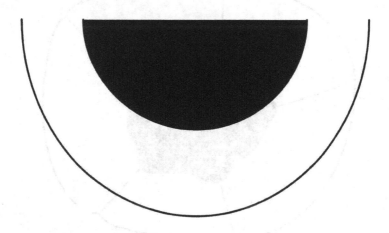

The wrong way to watch a 747 land.

The wrong way to watch a bullfight.

The wrong way to watch an
archery tournament.

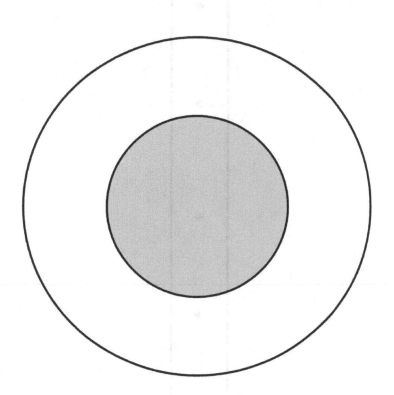

The wrong way to open a
bottle of champagne.

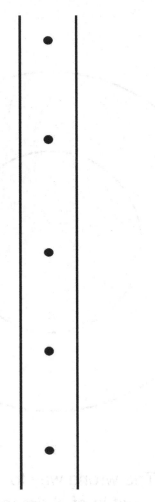

The wrong way to water the lawn.

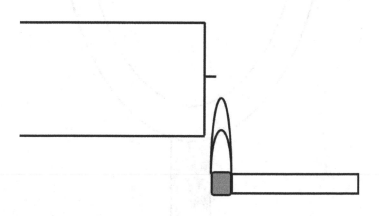

The wrong way to light a firecracker.

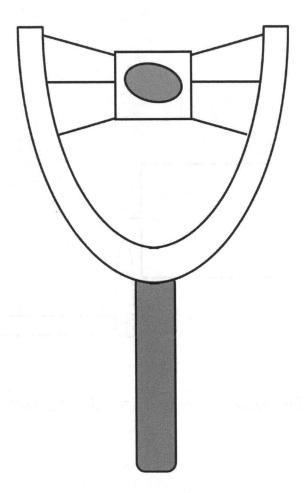

The wrong way to use a slingshot.

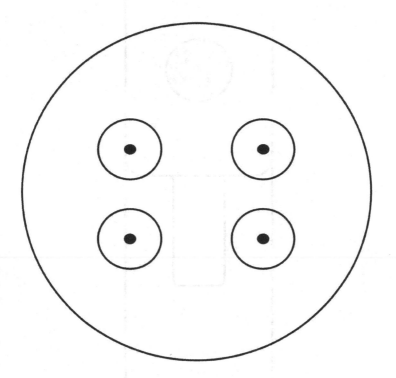

The wrong way to milk a cow.

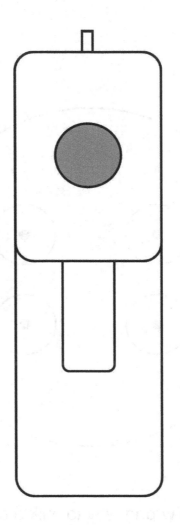

The wrong way to see if
your .45 is loaded.

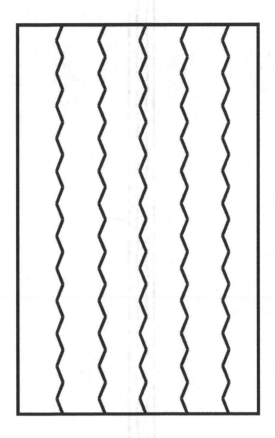

The wrong way to watch
the Indianapolis 500.

The wrong way to watch
the Tour de France.

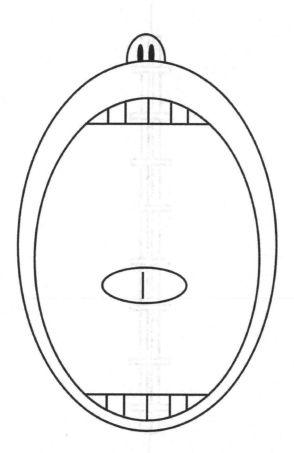

The wrong way to watch the opera.

The wrong way to block a punt.

The wrong way to watch ski jumping.

The wrong way to spray paint the house.

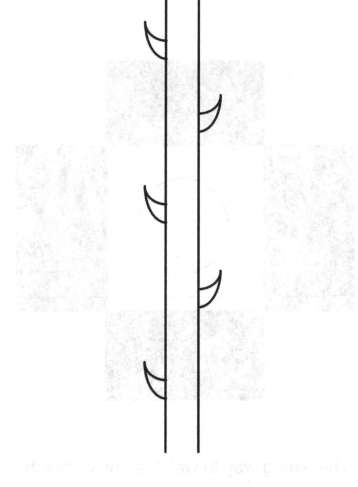

The wrong way to stop
and smell the roses.

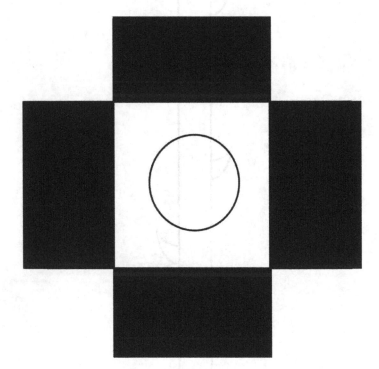

The wrong way to watch a chess match.

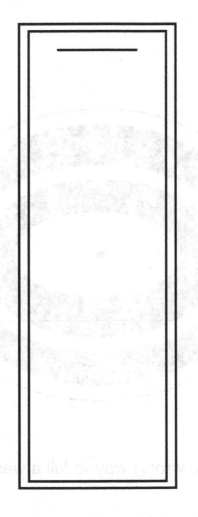

The wrong way to use a stapler.

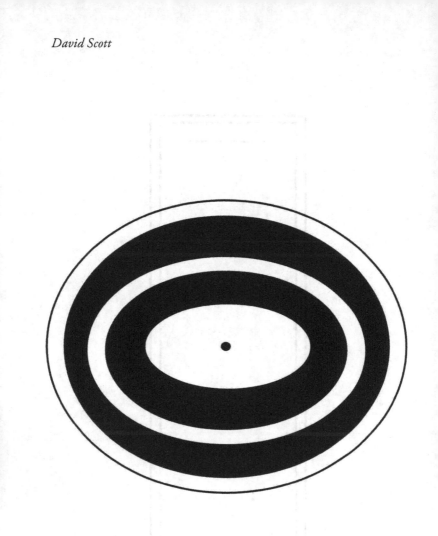

The wrong way to kill a wasp.

The wrong way to put in a contact lens.

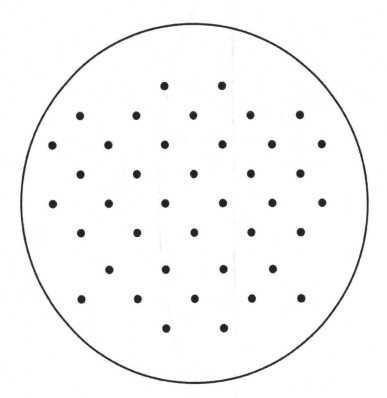

The wrong way to water the petunias.

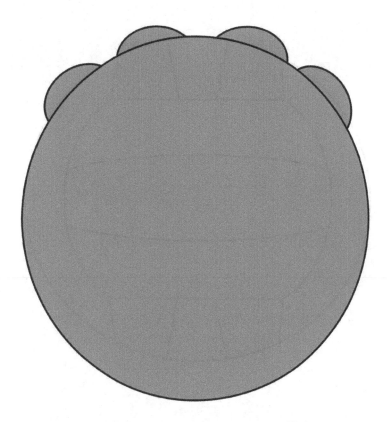

The wrong way to walk an elephant.

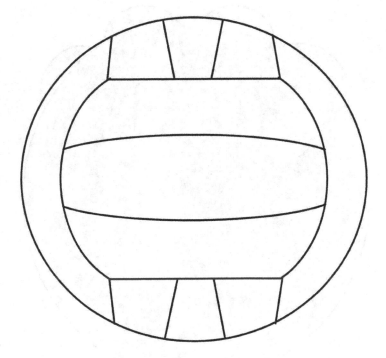

The wrong way to watch
a volleyball game.

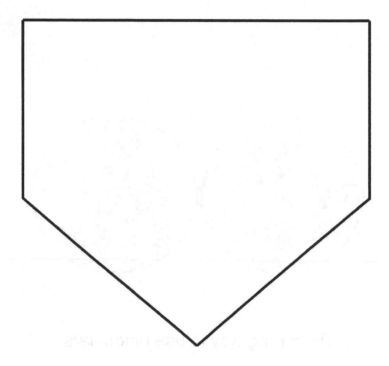

The wrong way to umpire
a baseball game.

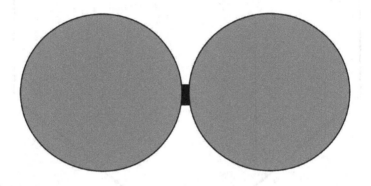

The wrong way to use binoculars.

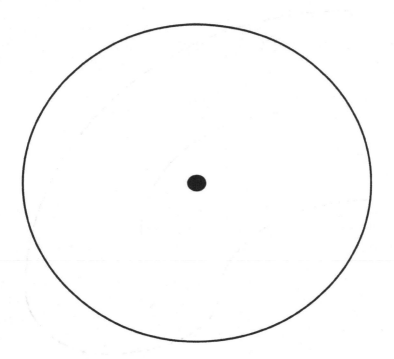

The wrong way to watch a
fencing tournament.

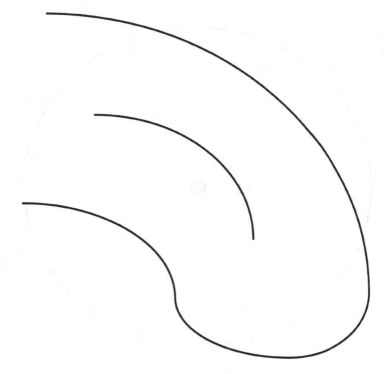

The wrong way to watch a
cat give itself a bath.

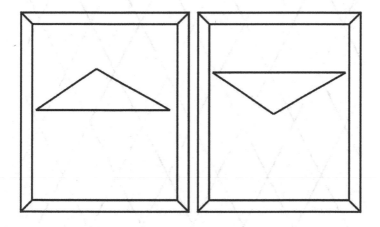

The wrong way to adjust the volume.

The wrong way to lie in a hammock.

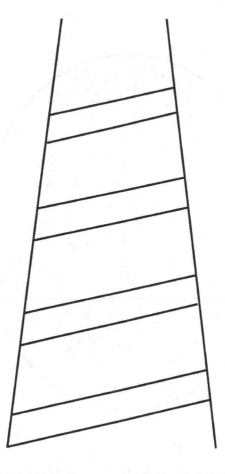

The wrong way to select a tie.

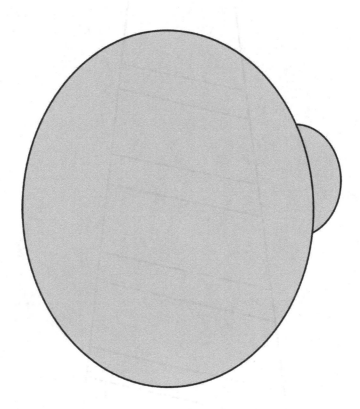

The wrong way to watch a boxing match.

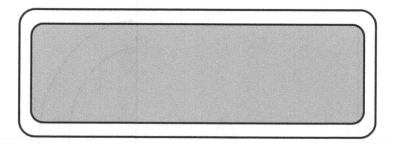

The wrong way to apply deodorant.

David Scott

The wrong way to drink coffee.

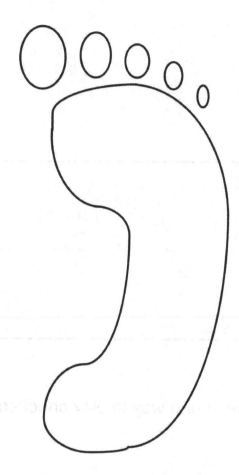

The wrong way to attend a
grape-crushing festival.

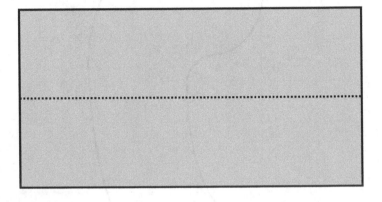

The wrong way to play checkers.

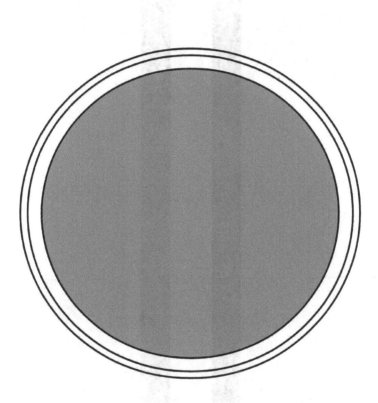

The wrong way to apply lipstick.

The wrong way to eat an Oreo.

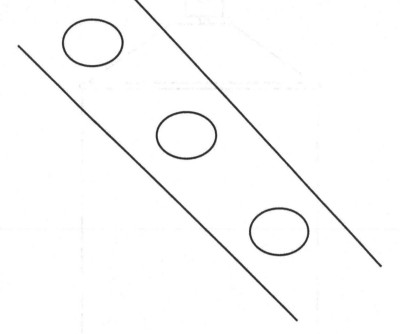

The wrong way to observe
a giant octopus.

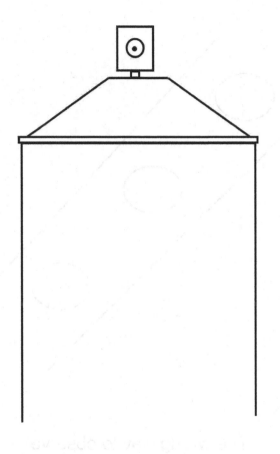

The wrong way to use hairspray.

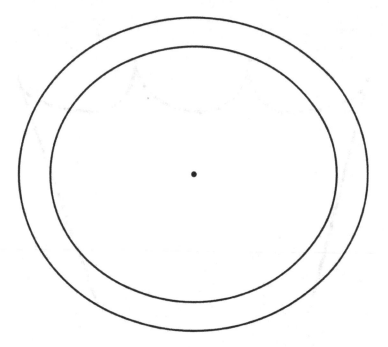

The wrong way to use a
hypodermic needle.

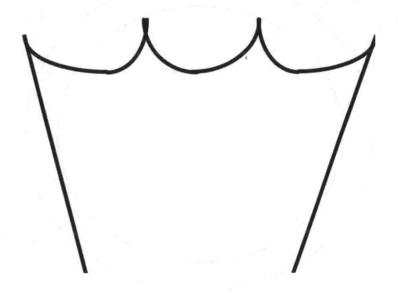

The wrong way to go duck hunting.

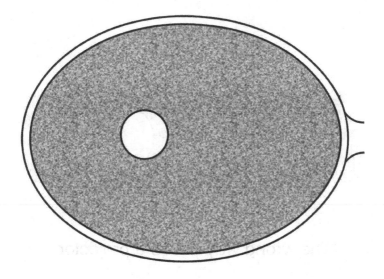

The wrong way to play ping pong.

The wrong way to use a projector.

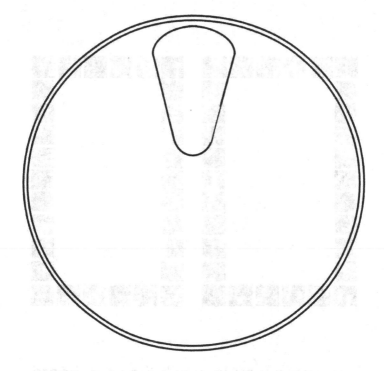

The wrong way to drink a Pepsi.

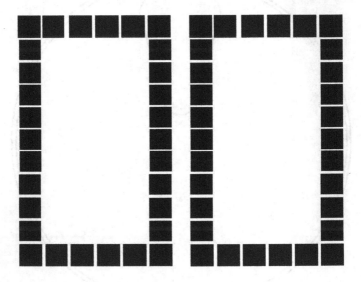

The wrong way to watch the scoreboard.

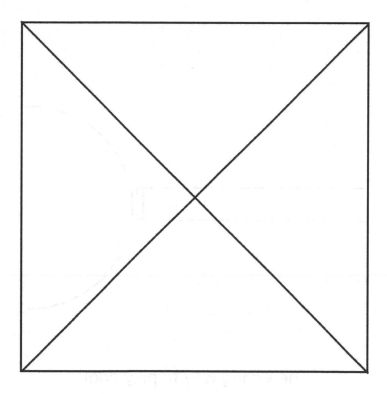

The wrong way to view the
Washington Monument

The wrong way to play pool.

The wrong way to go grouse hunting.

David Scott

The wrong way to stop a slap shot.

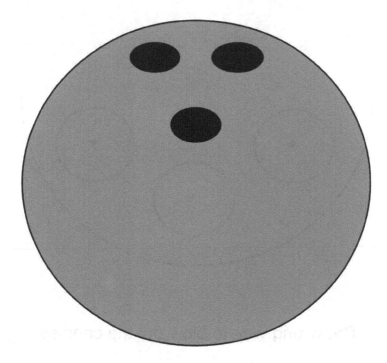

The wrong way to go bowling.

The wrong way to blow out the candles.

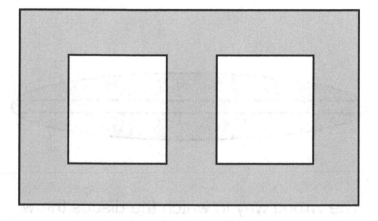

The wrong way to watch construction.

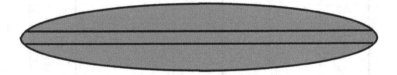

The wrong way to watch the discus throw.

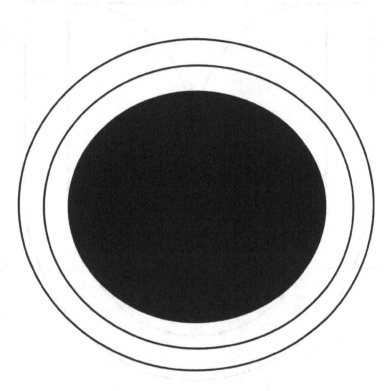

The wrong way to watch a fire fighter.

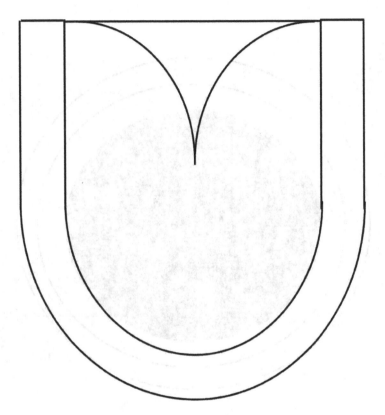

The wrong way to watch
the Kentucky Derby.

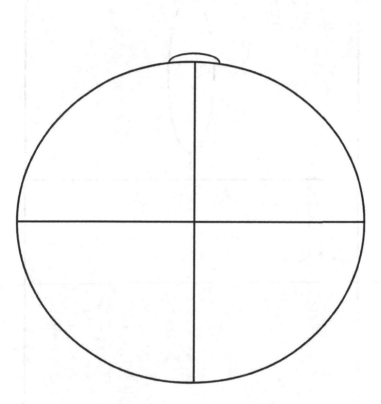

The wrong way to catch a pass.

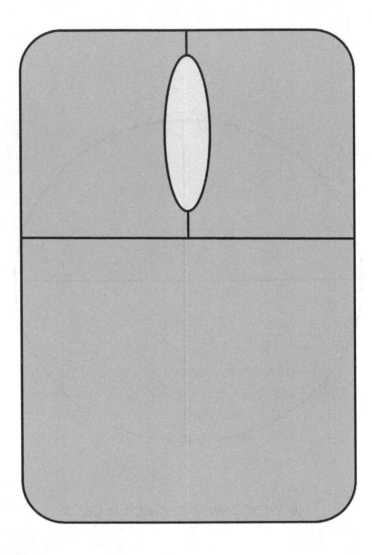

The wrong way to move a mouse.

The wrong way to play the piano.

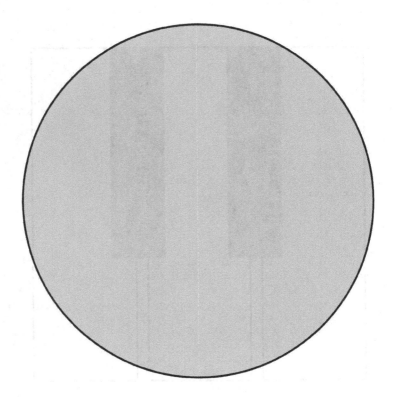

The wrong way to watch the
pole vault competition.

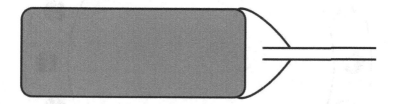

The wrong way to watch the
rowing competition.

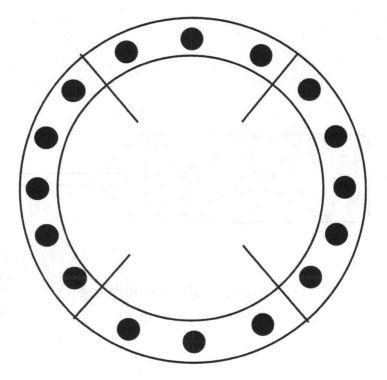

The wrong way to turn on the stove.

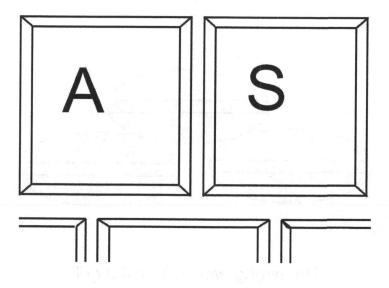

The wrong way to type a memo.

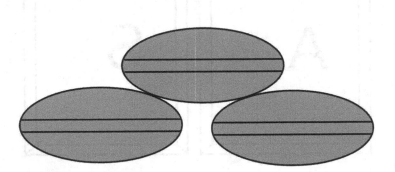

The wrong way to light the grill.

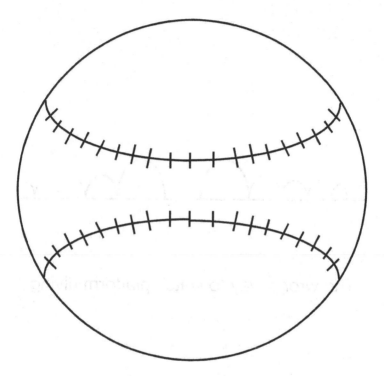

The wrong way to catch a line drive.

The wrong way to watch platform diving.

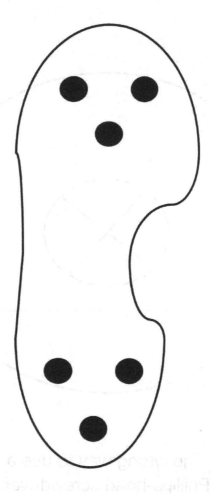

The wrong way to tackle a fullback.

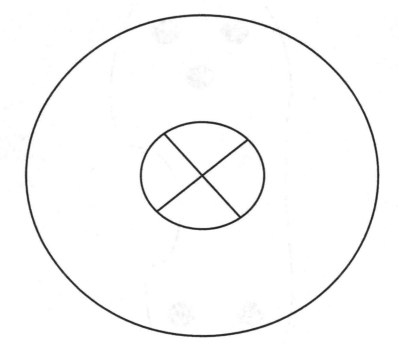

The wrong way to use a
Phillips-head screwdriver.

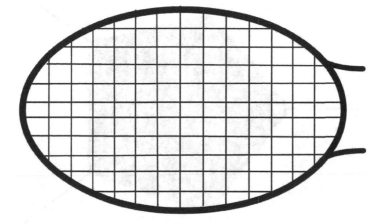

The wrong way to watch Wimbledon.

The wrong way to block a penalty kick.

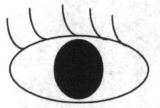
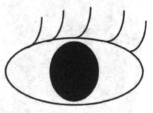

The wrong way to follow your
aerobics instructor.

The wrong way to watch a
shot put competition.

The wrong way to play the trumpet.

David Scott

The wrong way to catch a Frisbee.

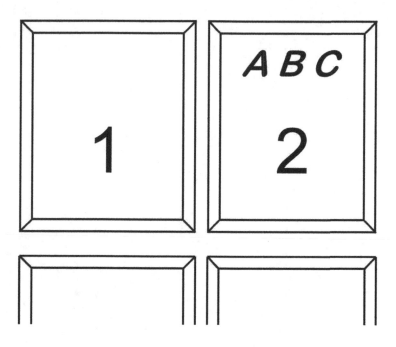

The wrong way to dial a phone.

The wrong way to visit Antarctica.

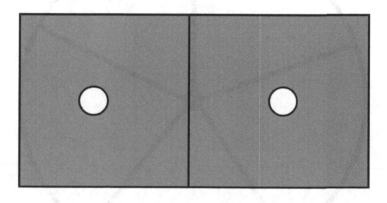

The wrong way to play dominos.

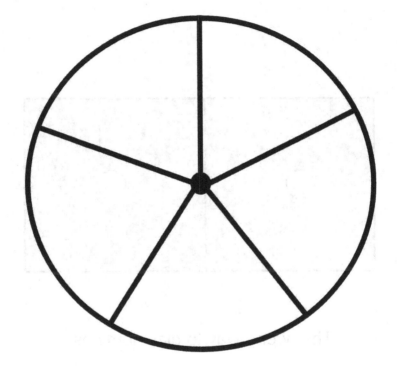

The wrong way to ski.

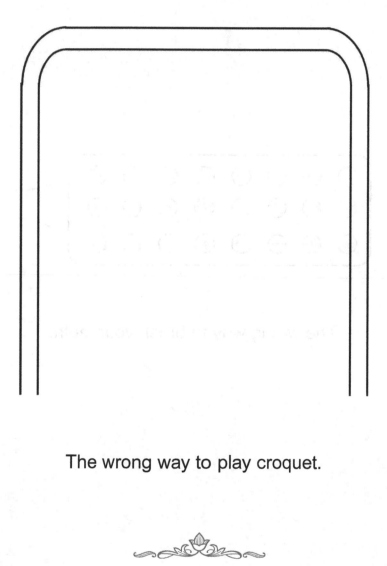

The wrong way to play croquet.

The wrong way to brush your teeth.

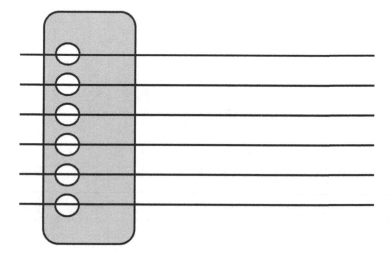

The wrong way to watch a rock concert.

ABOUT THE AUTHOR

David G. Scott has always had the ability to make people laugh—at work, in the classroom, or at the doctor's office. His older brother's prediction "Someday your mouth is going to write a check your body can't cash" has yet to happen.

As a boy, he saw a cartoon entitled a bear climbing a tree, which consisted of an upright rectangle in the middle of the page with four semicircles, two on either side of the rectangle. The bear was on the other side of the tree!

That idea rattled inside his brain for a long time and finally emerged as this book.

David lives in Kansas City with his wife and three offspring. They laugh with one another individually and, during family gatherings, they laugh together.

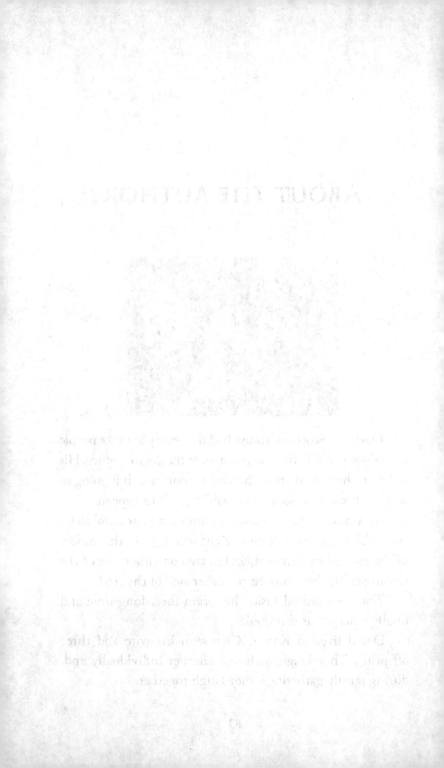

Printed in the United States
By Bookmasters